W9-APR-840

CAUSES OF WORLD WAR II

Causes of the American Revolution
Causes of the Civil War
Causes of World War I
Causes of World War II
Causes of the 1991 and 2003 Gulf Wars

CAUSES OF WORLD WAR II

Jim Corrigan

OTTN
PUBLISHING
STOCKTON, NJ

OTTN Publishing
16 Risler Street
Stockton, NJ 08859
www.ottnpublishing.com

First printing

1 3 5 7 9 8 6 4 2

Library of Congress Cataloging-in-Publication Data

  Corrigan, Jim.
    Causes of World War II / Jim Corrigan.
        p. cm. — (The road to war)
    Summary: "Discusses and explains the events of the 1920s and
1930s that led to the outbreak of the Second World War"—Provided
by publisher.
    Includes bibliographical references and index.
    ISBN-13: 978-1-59556-004-9
    ISBN-10: 1-59556-004-1
    ISBN-13: 978-1-59556-008-7 (pbk.)
    ISBN-10: 1-59556-008-4 (pbk.)
    1. World War, 1939-1945—Causes—Juvenile literature. I. Title. II.
Series.
    D741.C64 2006
    940.53'11—dc22

                                        2005006818

**Frontispiece: Nazi leader Adolf Hitler salutes marching German soldiers,
1938.**

TABLE OF CONTENTS

NOTABLE FIGURES

CHAMBERLAIN, NEVILLE (1869–1940). As Britain's prime minister, Arthur Neville Chamberlain was the chief architect of the disastrous policy of appeasement toward Adolf Hitler and the Nazis.

CHURCHILL, WINSTON (1874–1965). Considered Britain's greatest statesman of the 20th century, he was a vocal critic of the policy of appeasement before World War II; as prime minister from 1940 to 1945, he inspired and ably guided England in its war with the Axis Powers.

HIROHITO (1901–1989). After becoming Japan's emperor in 1926, Hirohito presided over an increasingly militaristic society—though he personally did not promote Japan's aggressive expansion.

HITLER, ADOLF (1889–1945). The Nazi leader exploited German dissatisfaction with the Versailles Treaty and with the Weimar Republic to become Germany's chancellor in 1933; after that, he assumed dictatorial powers, initiated a progressively more violent campaign against the Jews (which culminated in the Holocaust), and, through aggressions against European neighbors, set off World War II.

MUSSOLINI, BENITO (1883–1945). A former journalist, Mussolini masterfully used propaganda and mob violence to become Italy's prime minister in 1922; as the country's Fascist dictator, he ordered the conquest of Ethiopia, supported the Fascists under Francisco Franco during the Spanish Civil War, and allied Italy with Nazi Germany and, later, with Japan to form the Axis Powers.

Adolf Hitler

Franklin D. Roosevelt

Joseph Stalin

ROOSEVELT, FRANKLIN DELANO (1882–1945). Recognizing the Axis threat, the 32nd president of the United States ensured that the Allies received vital supplies, but isolationist sentiment kept the United States out of World War II until the Japanese attack on Pearl Harbor in December 1941.

STALIN, JOSEPH (1879–1953). The Soviet Union's longtime Communist dictator signed a nonaggression pact with Adolf Hitler in 1939; two years later, the Nazi invasion caught him by surprise, but the Soviet Union managed to recover and eventually drove the German armies back across eastern Europe to their final defeat in Berlin.

WILSON, WOODROW (1856–1924). After World War I, the 28th president of the United States advocated for a just and lasting peace (based on his Fourteen Points); however, he was unable to persuade the U.S. Senate to ratify the Versailles Treaty, so the United States did not join the League of Nations.

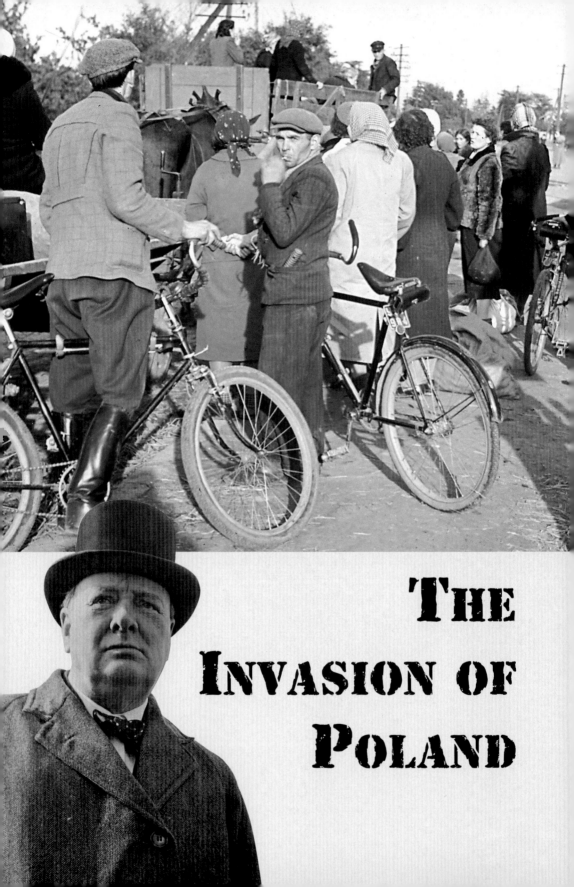

THE
INVASION OF
POLAND

Polish refugees clog the road near Warsaw during the German invasion of Poland, September 1939. During the 1930s, British statesman Winston Churchill (bottom left) was one of the few leaders concerned about a rearming Germany. His warnings proved to be correct, as Germany's military aggression led to the Second World War.

1

The year 1939 was a time of great anxiety in Europe. Germany was threatening neighboring nations with its awesome military power. Earlier in the year, German troops had marched into Czechoslovakia. As autumn approached, many people feared that Poland would become Germany's next victim.

Despite the anxiety, life in Poland's capital city of Warsaw went on normally. Citizens shopped for groceries, attended religious services, and strolled contentedly through the city's streets. Then, on a late summer day in 1939, everything suddenly changed. A series of explosions rocked the city. Warsaw was under attack by German bombers. In the streets, people ran in terror as windows shattered all about them.

On the outskirts of the city, small towns and villages were also being bombed. The people there thought it might be safer in Warsaw, so they grabbed their belongings and headed for the city. Upon arriving in Warsaw, they found it was much worse. Fires were burning everywhere and many buildings had been reduced to rubble. A number of people were killed while crossing a bridge that had been targeted by the German planes.

Within a month, Poland surrendered. Warsaw residents watched in despair as German troops marched through the streets. Soon the soldiers were giving orders, and anyone who did not obey was shot. Jewish families were forced to leave their homes and live in a guarded section of the city called the *ghetto*.

The invasion of Poland marked the beginning of World War II. After France and Britain declared war on the *Axis Powers*, the conflict spread quickly, engulfing most European nations. It broadened into Asia, where fighting between Japan and China was

A makeshift grave for Polish soldiers killed during the Nazi offensive. The poorly equipped Polish army was no match for Germany's tanks, mechanized infantry divisions, and dive-bombers.

already under way. The war soon became a global crisis, as neutral countries such as the United States and the Soviet Union were attacked. By the close of 1941, nearly every nation on Earth was embroiled in the conflict. When it finally ended in September 1945, some 55 million people had lost their lives.

World War II was caused by a series of unique events that occurred between 1919 and 1939. Ironically, the first of these events was the peace treaty that ended World War I. Rather than ensuring the peace, this document started the world down the road to another war.

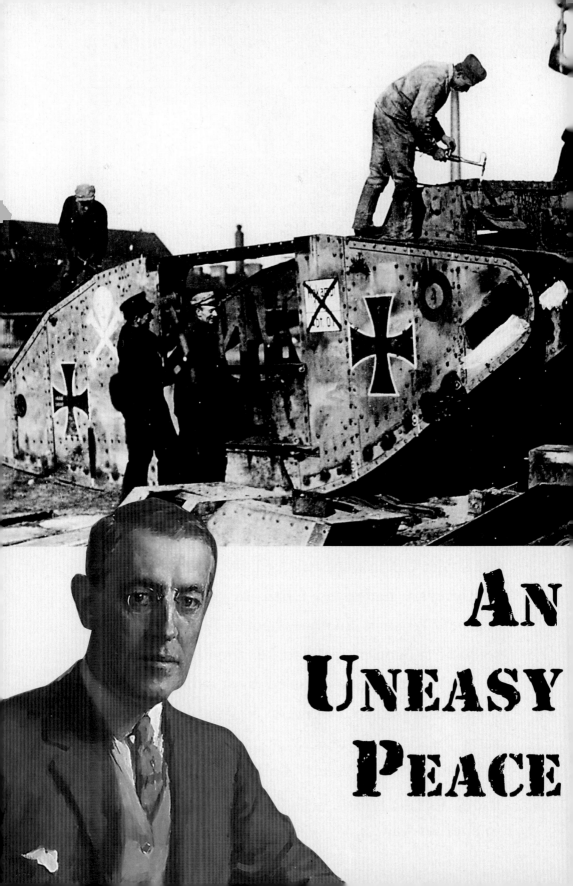

AN
UNEASY
PEACE

German workers destroy a World War I–era tank near Berlin, circa 1919. Woodrow Wilson (bottom left), the U.S. president, believed Germany should be treated fairly, but France and Britain wished to punish Germany for starting the First World War. Under the terms of the Treaty of Versailles, Germany was forced to reduce the size of its army and compensate the Allies for the cost of the war.

2

After the guns of World War I finally fell silent in November 1918, representatives from the warring countries gathered in Versailles, France, to plan for the future. The war had taken a tremendous toll in both money and human lives. The victorious nations, particularly France and Britain, were determined to punish the vanquished, namely Germany.

Woodrow Wilson, the U.S. president, attended the Versailles peace talks. It was the first time an American president had gone abroad while still in office, but Wilson knew the peace talks were important. He felt that a lasting peace could be achieved only if all countries were treated fairly. President Wilson proposed a plan he called the Fourteen Points. The plan included ideas such as freedom of the open seas, mutual weapons reduction, and freedom of trade. It also suggested redrawing certain boundaries in Europe and creating an international body called the League of Nations. Through the League, member nations could openly discuss issues with one another in order to prevent conflict.

Many of Wilson's points were adopted at the peace conference, but France and Britain still insisted on exacting revenge from Germany. Germany was forced to give up some of its European territory. France and Britain took Germany's overseas colonies for themselves. Additionally, Germany was ordered to pay monetary compensation for the cost of the war. Known as *reparations*, these costs came to $33 billion and were to be paid in the form of German ships, trains, money, and natural resources.

German leaders resented the heavy burden being placed on their country's war-ravaged economy, but

EUROPE, 1913

EUROPE, 1920

At the end of World War I, the victorious Allies redrew the borders of Europe, creating new countries like Yugoslavia and Czechoslovakia. Poland, which during the 18th century had been divided among Russia, Prussia (later part of Germany), and Austria, was reestablished as an independent country. German leaders were angry that a corridor of Polish territory separated East Prussia from the rest of Germany.

there was little they could do to stop it. Woodrow Wilson and some others at the conference also thought that the reparation demands being made of Germany were excessive. However, Wilson was more concerned that the negotiations lead to creation of the League of Nations, which they did.

When the peace treaty was finally signed on June 28, 1919, it was met with bitterness throughout Germany. Many German civilians refused to believe that their army had been defeated on the battlefield. Germany's military leaders had realized in early 1918 that the war could not be won, but they withheld that knowledge from the German public. And no foreign soldier had set foot on German soil. The surrender therefore came as a shock to most civilians. To accept defeat was difficult enough, but to accept responsibility for starting the war, and also be forced to pay reparations, seemed unthinkable.

The treaty also required Germany to disarm. The army would shrink to just 100,000 men armed with limited weapons. The navy would be reduced to 24 ships, and the air force would virtually disappear. These restrictions further angered a German populace who felt betrayed by their leaders.

Other nations resented the Treaty of Versailles as well. Italy and Japan had fought on the side of the victors, yet they received few rewards. Even Americans were dissatisfied. The United States had entered the war late, but American soldiers played an important role in bringing it to an end. Upon hearing of the lavish gains of France and Britain at Versailles, many Americans felt as if the war had been fought only to expand the French and British empires. To President Wilson's dismay, Congress refused to ratify the Treaty of Versailles. Accordingly, the United States never became a member of the League of Nations.

THE RISE OF FASCISM

The 1920s were a time of great uncertainty all over the world. The horror of World War I caused many people to question the principles of modern life. There was also widespread fear over a new style of government—*communism*. In 1917, Russia had undergone a revolution that ousted the Russian czar, or king. Eventually a Communist government gained power, and the nation that emerged came to be known as the Soviet Union.

Initially, the theory of communism held broad appeal, especially among the poor people of the world. Under communism, the government owns all property. Each person is supposed to labor for the good of the community, and everyone is supposed to share in the fruits of that labor. During the 1920s, political parties sprang up in most countries promoting the Communist way of life. However, as communism developed in the Soviet Union, it became clear that something had gone terribly wrong. Led by dictator Joseph Stalin, the Soviet government was cruel and oppressive. Harsh discipline, slave labor camps, and secret executions were the norm.

In Italy, there was considerable fear of communism. Additionally, Italians were frustrated by the outcome of World War I and the economic downturn that followed. A war veteran and former newspaperman named Benito Mussolini saw this unrest as an opportunity. Mussolini was a skilled public speaker and an expert at spreading *propaganda*. He began making speeches about defeating communism. He passed out pamphlets that talked about restoring the lost glory of Italy. Mussolini told the Italian people exactly what they wanted to hear.

Mussolini organized his followers into *fasci*, or groups. They were called "Fascists" and they all wore black shirts as a sign of unity. The Fascists attacked anyone who disagreed with them, especially Communists. By the fall of 1922, Mussolini had tens of thousands of black-shirted followers. They

Benito Mussolini gestures while speaking at a rally in the Coliseum of Rome, 1920. With the support of his black-shirted Fascist followers, Mussolini took control of Italy's government.

marched to Rome, the capital of Italy, and demanded that Mussolini be made Italy's prime minister. Fearing a rebellion, the king reluctantly agreed.

Once in power, Mussolini worked to turn Italy into a dictatorship. He bullied the parliament and censored the newspapers. He had his political opponents imprisoned or murdered. With fiery speeches and endless propaganda, he convinced most Italians that he was a modern-day Roman emperor. Those who did not agree with him were too afraid to say anything. In Fascism, Benito Mussolini had discovered a powerful new political system. Concepts such as personal freedom and individual rights were irrelevant. All that mattered was the glory of the state and its supreme leader. Fascism used lies to inspire its believers and terror to silence its critics.

GERMANY IN CRISIS

In the aftermath of the First World War, German emperor Wilhelm II was forced to relinquish power and flee the country. A new government emerged in his place. Founded in the town of Weimar, it came to be known as the Weimar Republic. The new government brought democracy to Germany. For the first time, the German people had the right to vote, freedom of speech, and many other important civil rights.

Despite its democratic ideals, the Weimar Republic was an unpopular government. Its foreign concepts were a constant reminder to many Germans that they had lost World War I. Further, the Weimar Republic was unable to solve Germany's worsening financial problems. Huge war debts to France and Britain were crushing the German economy.

The Weimar Republic responded to the financial crisis by printing vast amounts of new money. This only created high inflation, a problem in which money loses its value. In 1919, nine German marks equaled one American dollar. By 1922, it took 493 marks to equal one dollar. Like a runaway train, Germany's inflation rapidly sped out of control. By the end of 1923, it took 4.2 trillion marks to equal one dollar.

The financial crisis made life in Germany virtually impossible. A wheelbarrow full of money was needed just to buy a loaf of bread. Businesses used marks for notepaper because that was cheaper than buying a notepad. Theft became common as families stole food in order to survive. The Weimar Republic grew weak and helpless. People began calling for a new form of government.

In November 1923, a 34-year-old radical named Adolf Hitler decided to take action. He and 600 members of his Nazi Party stormed a political meeting in the city of Munich. They took several government officials hostage and declared that a national revolution had begun. The following morning, Hitler and 2,000 armed Nazis marched on the city's center. They clashed with police, and in the melee 16 Nazis were killed. Hitler was arrested and imprisoned for treason. His attempt at revolution had failed, but the incident stirred the imagination of the German people.

After serving less than a year of a five-year sentence, Hitler was released from prison. He reorganized the Nazi Party and worked to get Nazi candidates elected

"Hitler builds, we help," reads the inscription at the top of this Nazi propaganda poster. During the 1920s Adolf Hitler gained followers by pledging to build a glorious new Germany. His promises were attractive to Germans humiliated by the harsh terms of the Treaty of Versailles and frustrated with their country's economic problems.

to the German parliament. As economic conditions worsened, desperate Germans turned to Hitler and the Nazis for change. By 1933, Hitler held enough power to become Germany's chancellor, or chief minister. Before long, Nazis were running the entire government.

Like Mussolini, Hitler used the Fascist principles of lies and violence to gain power. But Hitler proved to be a far more ruthless dictator. While imprisoned in 1924, Hitler had written a book called *Mein Kampf* (My Struggle), which outlined his beliefs. In the book, he argued that German society needed to rid itself of what he deemed inferior peoples. While Mussolini spoke of restoring glory to the nation, Hitler emphasized the importance of "racial purity." Hitler believed that ethnic Germans were the leaders of what he called the Aryan (white) race. He felt that a society of "pure" Germans would ultimately rule Europe, and perhaps the world.

Hitler encouraged the use of propaganda to arouse racial hatred. He stated that the German people needed *lebensraum* (living space), which would have to be seized from neighboring nations by force. Hitler believed it was morally acceptable for the superior German civilization to take land from those he considered inferior. In 1933, as Germany's dictator, Hitler began putting his beliefs into practice.

IMPERIAL JAPAN

Japanese troops overrun Chinese defenders in Korea, 1894. Success in wars with China (1894–95) and Russia (1904–05) gave the military great influence over Japan's government. When Emperor Hirohito (bottom left) began appearing in public wearing a military uniform and carrying a sword, many Japanese believed the emperor supported the military and favored war.

3

World War I had devastated the countries of Europe, but for Japan it brought great fortune. Japanese factories thrived during the war by selling arms and supplies to Europe. Being a major trading power was a new role for Japan. Only 50 years earlier Japan had shunned modern technology and ideas.

Prior to 1868, Japan followed a strict policy of *isolationism.* Western ideas and beliefs were considered dangerous to

Japanese society, so contact with the Western world was limited. But by the mid-1800s, it was clear that isolationism would no longer work. Merchant ships from the United States, Britain, and other Western nations routinely appeared in Japanese harbors seeking trade. Japanese leaders came to realize that their nation had fallen behind technologically.

In 1868, the young emperor Meiji ascended to the throne. He ordered an end to isolationism. Japanese diplomats were sent to learn about the ways of other nations. The diplomats returned with new ideas about science, technology, and industry. Japan embarked on a program to catch up with the rest of the world. Factories were built, railroads were constructed, and new schools were established. Young men were drafted to serve in a new national military.

A NEW WORLD POWER

Japan's rising military and economic power led to tensions with its much larger neighbor, China. Japan could only expand its influence in the region at China's expense. In 1894, the two nations went to war over the Chinese *protectorate* of Korea. The modern Japanese army and navy easily defeated the ill-prepared Chinese forces. Japan forced China to recognize Korea's independence. As reparations for the war, China agreed to give Japan the island of Taiwan, plus the Liaotung Peninsula on the Chinese mainland. However, when Russia stepped into the negotiations and objected, Japan bitterly accepted money instead of the peninsula.

The Japanese resented Russia's interference in the peace negotiations with China. The Liaotung Peninsula was valuable land. Located in the Chinese region known as Manchuria, it contained an important naval base. When Russian troops moved into Manchuria a few years later, Japan decided to go to war.

Russia had a stronger military than China, but the Japanese fought fiercely. When Japan's navy destroyed a large number of Russian warships at the Battle of Tsushima in 1905, Russia negotiated for peace. There was much celebration when Japan finally received the Liaotung Peninsula.

The victory over Russia brought another benefit— Japan was recognized by the Western nations as a world power. When Japan *annexed* Korea in 1910, no other country complained. Following World War I, Japan became one of the founding members of the League of Nations. In 1922, Japanese delegates also attended the Washington Conference, at which each of the Pacific powers agreed to limit the size and number of its warships. The same nations also agreed to respect China's rights to self-government and free trade.

Although Japan enjoyed its new status as a leader in world affairs, at home things were no longer going so well. The nation's economy slowed dramatically after World War I because Europe no longer needed to buy Japanese war products. In 1923, a major earthquake struck the cities of Tokyo and Yokohama. It killed 140,000 people and flattened many factories. Unemployment and poverty rates climbed frighteningly high. The Japanese people blamed their politicians for the economic crisis. Several government officials were assassinated.

Many young officers within the Japanese military believed Japan needed to expand its empire. Colonies made a country powerful, these officers argued. Colonies contained land for farming, coal and oil to power factories, and people to buy Japanese goods.

The officers pointed to the vast empires of France and Britain and asked why Japan should not have the same. They reminded their leaders that Japan's previous aggression had successfully led to the annexation of Korea. Perhaps it was time for further aggression, they suggested. Despite these arguments, the emperor and his advisers were unconvinced. Seizing colonies would lead to war, they said, and war was the last thing Japan needed during this difficult time.

THE MILITARY TAKES OVER

As economic conditions worsened, the young officers gained more supporters in the military. Secret plans were made for the Japanese army to occupy the entire Manchurian region. But the army needed to invent an excuse before it could invade Chinese territory. On the night of September 18, 1931, Japanese soldiers posing as Chinese terrorists blew up the South Manchuria Railway. Pretending to be outraged by this imaginary act of Chinese sabotage, Japanese commanders ordered their troops to attack.

In Tokyo, the Japanese government was shocked to learn that its army was marching through Manchuria. The military had not asked for permission to attack. Government officials sent desperate messages ordering the army to halt. Those messages were ignored. Within a few months, Japanese troops occupied all of Manchuria.

The world condemned Japan's actions. The League of Nations investigated the Manchurian Incident, as the affair was called, and demanded that Japanese forces withdraw from Chinese soil at once. But the League could not enforce its demands. Japan simply refused to withdraw and cancelled its membership in the League of Nations. With no hope left of reclaiming

Japanese troops march into Manchuria, September 1931.

Manchuria, China signed a truce with Japan to end the fighting.

The army's success in Manchuria made it popular with the Japanese public. Gradually, the military took control of the government and the economy. Japan cast aside the agreements made at the Washington Conference and began building a huge navy. The army also grew larger and more powerful. Factories were instructed to produce war materials. Nearly all of Japan's precious natural resources were reserved for military purposes.

Under the military, Japan returned to a policy of isolationism. Propaganda constantly told the Japanese people that foreigners were inferior. Citizens were also told that they should concentrate only on being loyal to Japan and the emperor. Personal freedoms slowly vanished. The military government told each person where to work, how to behave, and what to think.

Japanese war planners began searching for their next conquest. China was a huge and tempting target. In July 1937, a skirmish broke out between Japanese soldiers and Chinese troops who were guarding the city of Beijing. The fighting escalated as more troops from each side arrived. But just as before, the Chinese were unable to stop the well-equipped Japanese soldiers. Within six months, Japan controlled a large swath of northern China.

The world again reacted with outrage at the latest Japanese aggression in China. However, no country was willing to get involved militarily. The United States protested by limiting its trade with Japan. This was a meaningful step because Japan depended on the U.S. for petroleum, steel, and other important goods. If the flow of these goods stopped entirely, the Japanese war machine would be threatened. Some Japanese leaders privately predicted that a confrontation with the United States would eventually be necessary.

GLOBAL DESPAIR

Adolf Hitler salutes his followers at a rally in Nuremberg, 1937. As Germany grew stronger economically and militarily under Hitler's rule, more Germans accepted Nazi ideology, including persecution of Jews. The Nazi soldier (bottom left) is holding a placard that says, "Germans Defend Yourselves! Don't buy from the Jews!"

The disturbing events taking place inside Germany and Japan went largely unnoticed by other nations. Despite the warning signs, few countries believed that the Nazis or the Japanese military posed a serious threat. Furthermore, most governments were distracted by a worldwide financial crisis during the 1930s. In Europe, they called it the Slump. In the United States, it came to be known as the Great Depression.

THE GREAT DEPRESSION

World War I transformed the United States into an economic giant. After the war, American factories switched from producing war supplies to manufacturing consumer goods. Wonderful new products such as automobiles, refrigerators, and washing machines were in great demand during the 1920s. Because the war had largely destroyed European industry, American products faced little competition. U.S. companies were soon making enormous profits. The prosperous decade was termed "the Roaring Twenties."

Problems were developing that would bring the Roaring Twenties crashing to an end. First, although some business owners were growing extremely wealthy, millions of workers were still being paid low wages. At the same time, these underpaid workers were being encouraged to borrow money so they could buy luxury goods. Soon many Americans found themselves deeply in debt.

American workers were not the only ones in debt. European governments borrowed money from American banks in order to rebuild after World War I. Among these governments was Germany's Weimar Republic. As conditions worsened in Germany, it became clear that the Weimar Republic would be unable to repay its

Jobless Americans line up at a government center distributing food and supplies in Arizona during the Great Depression.

debts. The American banks that had made the loans suffered heavy losses.

Few people realized just how fragile the U.S. economy had grown until the stock market crashed in October 1929. In the wake of steep losses, hundreds of factories were forced to close. Millions of workers were left jobless, unable to pay their debts or buy new products. Banks failed and stores went bankrupt. Farmers lost their land. Across the country, long lines of hungry people waited for free meals from soup kitchens.

Like a plague, the Great Depression spread around the globe. In some nations, one out of every three workers was unemployed. In countries such as Germany and Japan, which were already in crisis, people sank deeper into despair. They were drawn to radical groups, such as the Nazis, who promised to end their suffering and restore their country to glory. The Great Depression led millions of new believers to both Hitler and the Japanese militarists.

AXIS AGGRESSION

The rearmament of Germany and Japan occurred at a frantic pace during the mid-1930s. German factories produced large numbers of tanks and airplanes. In Japanese dockyards, the massive hulls of battleships and aircraft carriers were being assembled. Propaganda in both nations instructed civilians to work hard and live frugally, for food and resources needed to be saved for the military. In 1935, Hitler announced plans to expand the German army to more than 500,000 men.

A similar rearmament took place in Italy under Benito Mussolini, but on a smaller scale. By October 1935, Mussolini was ready to test his army's abilities. Italy invaded the African nation of Ethiopia. The goal was to turn Ethiopia into an Italian colony. Mussolini ignored protests by the League of Nations and continued his attack. In the spring of 1936, Italy annexed Ethiopia.

Hitler was impressed by Mussolini's daring conquest. The dictators began working together on common goals. When civil war erupted in Spain, they both sent troops to support the Fascist leader Francisco Franco. They signed a pact vowing to fight communism. Other European nations began to worry about the powerful alliance between Germany and Italy.

Meanwhile, shocking stories about Japanese atrocities in China were beginning to emerge. In December

Ethiopian leader Haile Selassie asks the League of Nations for help during Italy's 1935–36 invasion of his country. The League had been formed to prevent warfare, but whenever a nation was condemned for aggressive behavior, that nation simply withdrew from the organization and continued its aggression. Germany and Japan withdrew from the League of Nations in 1933, and Italy withdrew in 1937. By 1940, the League struggled merely to remain in existence.

1937, Japanese troops overran the walled city of Nanjing. They then went on a six-week-long rampage of looting, torture, and murder. The Japanese did not just execute the Chinese soldiers they took prisoner. They also murdered civilians, including the elderly, women, and children. Some were beheaded, some burned to death, some buried alive. In addition, thousands of women and girls were sexually assaulted. No one knows exactly how many Chinese were killed during the notorious "Rape of Nanjing." Estimates of the death toll range from 50,000 to 250,000 or more Chinese.

Burned and abandoned, a Chinese infant wails on a railroad platform in Shanghai moments after a Japanese air raid, 1937. As Japan pressed its invasion of China, Japanese troops committed numerous atrocities against Chinese civilians.

By 1938, Hitler was ready to implement his plan to control Europe. His first step was called *Anschluss*, or unification, with neighboring Austria. Six million ethnic Germans lived in Austria, and Hitler said he wanted them to be reunited with German society. In March 1938, German troops marched into Vienna, the Austrian capital. Many Austrians welcomed the Germans. After years of suffering economic hardships, they saw Hitler as a powerful new force in the world. They were pleased to become part of Germany's *Third Reich*.

HATE AND FEAR INSIDE THE AXIS

Nazi aggression was not just directed outward at other countries. It was also directed inward at German society. In order to carry out his plans, Hitler needed absolute loyalty. He recognized that hate is a powerful emotion, so Hitler and the Nazis used hate as a tool to inspire loyalty and attract new followers.

Throughout the 1930s, the Nazis tightened their grip on German society. They used modern technology such as radio and film to spread propaganda. They organized rallies to burn books that were said to be "un-German." They even held elaborate public ceremonies that gave Nazism the appearance of a religion. Hitler and other Nazi leaders were idolized.

Organizations like the Hitler Youth taught Nazi beliefs and values to young people in the Third Reich.

No part of German society was overlooked, including children. Nazi beliefs were taught in schools, and young boys were drafted into an organization called the Hitler Youth. Females joined the League of German Girls. Youth groups such as these emphasized military-like discipline and absolute loyalty to Adolf Hitler.

The Nazis developed a definition of what they considered to be the ideal German. Anyone who did not meet this definition—including Jews, Gypsies, Communists, and homosexuals—was ridiculed. Hitler blamed the Jewish population in particular for Germany's problems. The Nazis taught that Jews had been responsible for the Treaty of Versailles, the financial crisis of the 1920s, and the failure of the Weimar Republic. Government-sponsored hatred of Jews increased dramatically during the 1930s.

Germany's Nazism, Italy's Fascism, and Japan's imperialism were all unique political movements. However, they did share certain common features. Hitler, Mussolini, and Hirohito were all worshipped with god-like reverence. Propaganda in each nation encouraged aggressive behavior toward foreigners and blind loyalty to the ruling party. Rational thought was discouraged because it exposed the many flaws and contradictions in the ruling party's beliefs. Each country had secret-police organizations that hunted down dissenters. During a three-year period in Japan, more than 60,000 people were arrested for having "dangerous thoughts." In Germany, the feared *Gestapo* maintained order with secret torture and executions.

Although there were many instances of heroic resistance, most citizens of the Axis nations either succumbed to the propaganda or remained silent out of fear. With complete control over their populations, the Axis leaders were free to proceed with their plans for the building of empires.

Mixed reactions to Germany's seizure of the Sudeten-land in September 1938. (Background) Sudeten German girls wearing traditional costumes salute enthusiastically during a speech welcoming Hitler. (Inset) A Czech woman, compelled to salute, weeps uncontrollably as Nazi soldiers march past.

5

SLIPPING INTO WAR

The danger posed by the Axis Powers slowly became clear to France and Britain. They were particularly alarmed by the power of the rebuilt German military. In just two decades, Germany had transformed itself from a beaten nation into an awesome military power.

The rearmament was a blatant violation of the Treaty of Versailles. But France and Britain had been too distracted holding their far-flung empires together to notice. By 1938, the time had passed for preventing the buildup—Germany was too powerful to control. Even worse, France and Britain had cut back on military spending since World War I. They would need to rearm quickly in order to catch up with Germany.

Britain's new prime minister, Neville Chamberlain, did not believe another war would be necessary. Chamberlain thought that Germany could be pacified by negotiations. He recognized that the Treaty of Versailles had been unfair. He also thought that the German leader, Adolf Hitler, was a novice who could be easily duped at the bargaining table. Accordingly, Chamberlain employed a strategy of *appeasement*. He would indulge Hitler's demands, hoping that eventually the German dictator would become satisfied.

Once Germany annexed Austria in March 1938, some European leaders felt that German aggression would end. Others cautioned that it was only the beginning. A British politician named Winston Churchill frequently gave speeches and wrote newspaper columns about the Nazi menace. His warnings gained credibility in the summer of 1938, when Germany began threatening Czechoslovakia.

THE MUNICH CONFERENCE

Like Austria, Czechoslovakia contained a large population of ethnic Germans. These Germans were concentrated in a western area of Czechoslovakia known as the Sudetenland. Hitler demanded that Czechoslovakia cede the Sudetenland to Germany. When Czechoslovakia refused, Hitler spoke of war.

Britain and France urged the Czechs to appease Hitler. Accordingly, Czechoslovakia gave the Sudetenland Germans new rights and freedoms. But Hitler was not satisfied. He demanded that Czechoslovakia give up the Sudetenland entirely. The outbreak of war seemed very close.

Britain's Neville Chamberlain was certain that he could reason with Hitler. He took the bold step of flying to Germany for a face-to-face meeting. Hitler bluntly told Chamberlain that he was prepared to go to war over the Sudetenland. Hitler then offered a deal. He said that if the Czechs agreed to give him the Sudetenland, he would promise not to attack the remainder of Czechoslovakia in the future.

Britain and France implored the Czechs to accept Hitler's offer. Feeling that they had no other alternative, the Czechs reluctantly agreed. But just when it seemed the crisis had been averted, Hitler made another demand. He said that not only would the Czechs have to give up the Sudetenland, they would also have to give Germany additional territory. The deal was off and war once again seemed inevitable.

At this point, Benito Mussolini stepped in. He suggested that Britain, France, Germany, and Italy hold a conference to discuss the crisis. So in September 1938, the leaders of the four powers gathered in

Munich, Germany. Although the issue to be discussed was land that legally belonged to Czechoslovakia, the Czechs were not invited. During the meeting, Hitler spoke fervently about Germany's right to the Sudetenland. Mussolini supported his fellow dictator's claims. At the end of the conference, a pact was signed granting Germany the Sudetenland. In exchange, Hitler guaranteed an end to German aggression.

A grateful public greeted Chamberlain as he returned to Britain. The prime minister proudly waved the Munich Pact in the air and said that it represented "peace for our time." Hitler departed Munich with a completely different impression. He was convinced that Britain and France were weak and would avoid war at all costs. He ordered the Wehrmacht (the German army) and Luftwaffe (the German air force) to prepare for an assault on the remainder of Czechoslovakia. In March 1939, just six months after the Munich Conference, German tanks rolled into Czech territory. Hitler had broken his promise of peace. It would not be the last time he did so.

JAPAN EXPANDS INTO THE PACIFIC

The volatile situation in Europe drew attention away from Japanese aggression in Asia. Japanese troops continued to press deep into China, and by

Prime Minister Neville Chamberlain holds up a copy of the Munich Pact shortly after returning to Britain from the Munich Conference. "We regard the agreement signed last night . . . as symbolic of the desire of our two peoples never to go to war with one another again," Chamberlain said. "I believe it is 'peace for our time.' "

1939 they had reached the country's rugged interior. However, the jagged Chinese mountains proved to be a difficult place to fight. The Japanese invasion slowed to a halt.

With the war in China stalled, Japan began looking elsewhere to expand its empire. Important war materials such as oil and rubber were in short supply. Any country that possessed those resources would make an excellent colony. The region known as French Indochina (which today consists of Vietnam, Cambodia, and

Laos) was rich in natural resources. Many of the islands in the Pacific Ocean were also targeted.

Japanese leaders began planning what they called the "Greater East Asia Co-Prosperity Sphere." They described it as an association of Asian nations, led by Japan, that would cooperate economically and politically. In reality, Japan merely wanted these nations as colonies. The goal was to create an empire with enough natural resources to keep Japan strong. The citizens of these colonies would be soldiers and laborers, with the fruits of their efforts being sent back to Japan.

The United States watched Japan's actions in the Pacific warily. Japanese aggression could eventually threaten America's Pacific interests, such as the Philippine and Hawaiian Islands. Franklin D. Roosevelt, the U.S. president, wanted to stop Japan's aggression in the Pacific, but he could not do so militarily. The U.S. armed forces had been reduced considerably during the Great Depression. Furthermore, the American public was strongly opposed to fighting a war, either in Europe or the Pacific.

The United States and Japan began negotiating to resolve their differences, but those negotiations broke down when Japanese troops moved into French Indochina. In response, Roosevelt halted all U.S. petroleum shipments to Japan. Without American oil,

Japanese warships, aircraft, and ground forces would soon run out of fuel. Negotiations between the two countries resumed, but Japanese war planners quietly began drafting a plan to attack the United States.

THE INVASION OF POLAND

Britain and France were outraged by Germany's occupation of Czechoslovakia. Hitler had lied to them at Munich, and clearly he was bent on conquering Europe. The two nations decided to make a stand

DENMARK

Baltic Sea

DANZIG

GERMANY

North Sea

NETHERLANDS

•Berlin

•Warsaw

POLAND

GERMANY

BELGIUM

•Prague

CZECHOSLOVAKIA

LUX.

Vienna •

•Budapest

FRANCE

AUSTRIA

HUNGARY

N
W   E
S

SWITZERLAND

0   Miles   200

ITALY

German Aggression, 1936–1939
- German advance into the Rhineland, March 1936
- Anschluss with Austria, March 1938
- Occupation of Sudetenland, October 1938
- Occupation of Czechoslovakia, March 1939
- Conquest of Poland, September 1939

Aggression by other countries
- Occupied by Poland, 1938
- Occupied by Hungary, 1938–1939
- Occupied by the Soviet Union, 1939
- Slovakia, created March 1939

German and Soviet diplomats sign a non-aggression treaty, August 1939. The two countries secretly agreed to divide Poland.

against German aggression. The country of Poland, to the east of Germany, would likely be Hitler's next target. Britain and France stated that if Germany attacked Poland, they would come to Poland's aid.

Hitler regarded the British and French warnings as idle threats. He was certain that he could invade Poland without any interference from these weak, peace-loving nations. The Soviet Union was a different matter. Soviet dictator Joseph Stalin might be angered by an invasion so close to his territory. The

Soviet Red Army was large and powerful. Provoking it was a risk Hitler could not afford to take.

In August 1939, German and Soviet diplomats met secretly to discuss a treaty between their two countries. Germany wanted Soviet approval to invade Poland. The Soviets wanted assurances that they would not be attacked by Germany. The diplomats also agreed that their nations would share the spoils of victory in Poland and support one another during future aggressions in Eastern Europe. By signing the Nazi-Soviet Pact, Stalin believed he had prevented German aggression against his country. For Hitler, the pact meant that nothing stood between him and Poland.

On September 1, 1939, German bombers flew east and destroyed Poland's railways. They were followed by more than a million German troops, who surged across the border. The Polish army could do little to stop the attack. The German forces were using a new style of warfare called *blitzkrieg*, or lightning war. It combined precision air strikes with fast-moving troops and tanks. Blitzkrieg was the opposite of the trench warfare of World War I, and Poland crumbled beneath it.

To Hitler's amazement, Britain and France kept their word. On September 3, 1939, they declared war on Germany. World War II had begun.

The wreckage of a bus leans into a huge crater in front of bombed-out buildings in London. By September 1940 Germany had conquered most of Western Europe and had launched a devastating aerial bombardment of military and civilian targets within England.

6

WORLD CONFLICT

The first year of the war was disastrous for the French and British, who had joined forces as the *Allies*. The German blitzkrieg seemed unstoppable. It devoured smaller nations such as Luxembourg, Belgium, and the Netherlands. Hitler then turned his attention to France. The Allies tried to defend France with the obsolete tactics of World War I, which were useless against the blitzkrieg. By the end of June 1940, France was in German hands and Hitler was preparing for an invasion of Britain. At this point, Italy entered the war against the Allies.

Britain urged the United States to join the fight, but American public opinion was still passionately opposed to war. Most Americans viewed the war as a strictly European problem. President Roosevelt, however, was very sympathetic toward the Allies. He began lending American ships, weapons, and supplies to Britain. U.S. aid helped Britain survive the continuous German attack from air and sea.

In June 1941, Hitler initiated the largest struggle of the war. He broke his peace pact with Joseph Stalin and sent 3 million German troops into the Soviet Union. Stalin was so unprepared for the attack that during the first few hours he did not believe reports that it was occurring. Soviet troops retreated in chaos from the massive German invasion force. German soldiers moved deep inside Soviet territory before the Red Army could slow them down.

Meanwhile, Japan continued enlarging its empire in the Pacific. The United States protested, but those objections were ignored. Japanese leaders believed the strong antiwar feelings of the American people would prevent Roosevelt from taking military action against Japan. Further, they concluded that a crippling strike on U.S. forces in the Pacific might force Roosevelt to accept Japan's new empire.

On December 7, 1941, Japanese bombers and torpedo planes launched a surprise attack on the American naval fleet at Pearl Harbor, Hawaii. Similar assaults were made on American bases in the

Philippines, Guam, Wake Island, and elsewhere in the Pacific. Thousands of Americans were killed, wounded, or taken prisoner.

The surprise attacks produced the opposite effect of what Japan had intended. Americans were infuriated, and the United States committed itself to destroying the Japanese empire. In response, Germany and Italy also declared war on America, and the United States formally joined the Allies. Every major power was now embroiled in the conflict.

Smoke and flames surround the American battleships *West Virginia* and *Tennessee*, December 7, 1941. The surprise Japanese attack on Pearl Harbor forced the United States to enter World War II on the side of the Allies.

REVERSAL OF FORTUNES

America's entry into the war marked an important turning point. Once fully mobilized, U.S. industry and labor would give the Allies a decisive advantage. By early 1942, the tide was starting to turn against Germany. The drive into Soviet territory had stalled, and the fight against the Red Army slowly began draining German resources. Additionally, the British were beating Mussolini's Italian forces in North Africa, forcing Hitler to send troops in support of his ally.

In the Pacific, the United States embarked on a massive naval campaign against Japan. American aircraft carriers had survived the raid on Pearl Harbor. They now clashed with Japanese carriers at the Battle of the Coral Sea and the Battle of Midway. U.S. Marines began landing on Japanese-held islands, and vicious jungle fighting ensued. American submarines gradually severed the vital flow of Japanese supplies across the Pacific, slowing Japan's war production.

By 1944, the Axis forces were on the run. American and British soldiers had pushed through North Africa and landed in southern Italy. Soviet troops were driving the German invaders back. Japanese losses in the Pacific were also mounting as American troops captured island after island.

On June 6, 1944, the Allies launched Operation Overlord, also known as the D-Day landing. More than 175,000 Allied soldiers crossed the English Channel and stormed the coast of France. As these forces fought inland toward Germany from the west, Russian troops attacked from the east.

Unable to bear this vise-like pressure, Germany's Third Reich collapsed 11 months later. Facing capture, Adolf Hitler committed suicide in April 1945. Italy also surrendered. Benito Mussolini was tried and executed by his countrymen. His lifeless body was hung in a public square before jeering crowds.

The Japanese continued fighting until August 1945, when American planes dropped two atomic bombs over Japanese cities. The utter devastation wrought on Hiroshima and Nagasaki by these blasts persuaded Emperor Hirohito to surrender. Afterward, Hirohito was allowed to retain the title of emperor, but American officials transformed Japan into a democracy. Germany and Italy were also rebuilt as democracies.

In the decades since the end of World War II, a multitude of wars have been waged. But all of these conflicts have remained localized. Leaders of the most powerful nations recoil at the prospect of another no-holds-barred war like the one that began in 1939.

1919: The Treaty of Versailles is signed in June. The peace settlement imposes harsh penalties on Germany. Some victorious nations, such as Italy and Japan, are also dissatisfied with the treaty.

1920: The League of Nations is created with the goal of resolving future international disputes peacefully.

1921: Adolf Hitler becomes the leader of the Nazi Party as Germany sinks into financial crisis.

1922: Benito Mussolini become's prime minister of Italy.

1923: In September, a massive earthquake destroys Japan's industrial center, causing economic hardship. In November, a Nazi uprising in Munich fails to overthrow the German government.

1926: Emperor Hirohito ascends to the throne of Japan.

1929: The U.S. stock market crashes in October, heralding the start of the Great Depression.

1931: The Japanese military begins its long war of aggression in China with the invasion of Manchuria.

1933: The Nazis obtain control of the German government as Hitler is named chancellor in January. Persecution of German Jews begins. Japan and Germany withdraw from the League of Nations.

1935: Italy invades the African nation of Ethiopia.

1937: Fighting in China escalates as Japanese forces push deep into Chinese territory. Italy withdraws from the League of Nations.

1938: German troops enter Austria in March. During the summer, Hitler threatens to invade Czechoslovakia. At the Munich Conference in September, Britain and France agree to let Hitler have a portion of Czechoslovakia known as the Sudetenland. In exchange, Hitler promises peace.

1939: In March, Germany invades the remainder of Czechoslovakia. In August, Germany and the

Soviet Union sign a non-aggression pact. On September 1, Germany attacks Poland. In response, Britain and France declare war on Germany on September 3. World War II has begun.

1940: Germany invades France in May, forcing it to surrender on June 22. During the Battle of Britain, the Luftwaffe and the Royal Air Force battle for control of the skies.

1941: On June 22, Germany invades the Soviet Union. On December 7, Japan launches a surprise attack on Pearl Harbor. The next day, the United States declares war.

1942: In June, the Allies win a major victory in the Pacific at the Battle of Midway.

1943: The Italian government strips Mussolini of power and orders him arrested in July. On September 3, the Allies invade southern Italy; five days later Italy signs an armistice. However, German troops continue to resist the Allies in Italy. In the Pacific, the Allies recapture the Solomon Islands.

1944: On June 6 ("D-Day"), the Allies launch Operation Overlord. In the largest seaborne invasion in history, more than 175,000 Allied soldiers cross the English Channel and storm the coast of France.

1945: As American and Russian armies advance, the Third Reich collapses. Adolf Hitler commits suicide on April 30, and Germany surrenders on May 8. In Italy, Benito Mussolini is tried and executed by his countrymen. The Japanese prepare for an American invasion of their home islands. However, after atomic bombs are dropped on Hiroshima and Nagasaki, Japan surrenders on August 14.

GLOSSARY

ALLIES—the coalition of Britain, France, the United States, and many other nations that fought together to defeat the Axis Powers.

ANNEX—to join or take under control.

APPEASEMENT—the failed policy followed by Britain and France during the 1930s to maintain peace. It assumed that Hitler would be satisfied once certain German demands were met.

AXIS POWERS—the coalition of aggressor nations that included Germany, Italy, and later Japan.

BLITZKRIEG—German for "lightning war," it was a fast-moving attack with air power and ground forces designed to overwhelm enemy defenses.

COMMUNISM—a political system under which the government owns all property and each person is supposed to labor for the good of the community.

GESTAPO—Nazi Germany's secret police.

GHETTO—a walled, crowded section of town where Jews were forced to live before being deported to Nazi concentration camps.

ISOLATIONISM—a policy of avoiding contact with other nations.

LEBENSRAUM—German for "living space," it was Hitler's idea that the German people needed large tracts of land in order to grow and flourish. The land would be taken from other nations by force, if necessary.

PROPAGANDA—information and ideas that are spread in order to shape public opinion. The information is often misleading or false.

PROTECTORATE—a sovereign nation that is influenced and protected by a more powerful nation.

REPARATIONS—payments for the cost of war damages.

THIRD REICH—the name of the German empire while under Hitler's control.

BOOKS FOR STUDENTS:

Barr, Gary. *Pearl Harbor.* Chicago: Heinemann Library, 2004.

Giblin, James Cross. *The Life and Death of Adolf Hitler.* New York: Clarion Books, 2002.

Mulvihill, Margaret. *Mussolini and Italian Fascism.* New York: Franklin Watts, 1990.

Perl, Lila. *Behind Barbed Wire: The Story of Japanese-American Internment During World War II.* New York: Benchmark Books, 2002.

Ross, Stewart. *Causes and Consequences of World War II.* Chicago: Raintree, 1995.

Warren, Andrea. *Surviving Hitler: A Boy in the Nazi Death Camps.* New York: HarperCollins Publishers, 2001.

BOOKS FOR OLDER READERS:

Brendon, Piers. *The Dark Valley: A Panorama of the 1930s.* New York: Alfred A. Knopf, 2000.

Chang, Iris. *The Rape of Nanking: The Forgotten Holocaust of World War II.* New York: Basic Books, 1997.

Lamb, Margaret, and Nicholas Tarling. *From Versailles to Pearl Harbor: The Origins of the Second World War in Europe and Asia.* New York: Palgrave MacMillan, 2001.

Rothwell, Victor. *The Origins of the Second World War.* Manchester, UK: Manchester University Press, 2002.

Spielvogel, Jackson J. *Hitler and Nazi Germany: A History*, 4th edition. Englewood Cliffs, N.J.: Prentice Hall, 2000.

INTERNET RESOURCES

HTTP://WWW.USHMM.ORG/OUTREACH/POWER.HTM

This site describes how Hitler and the Nazis were able to seize power in Germany.

HTTP://WWW.SCHOOLSHISTORY.ORG.UK/EUROPEATWAR/INDEX.HTM

Interesting facts about prewar Europe, including the military readiness of each nation in 1939.

HTTP://HISTORY.ACUSD.EDU/GEN/WW2TIMELINE/PRELUDE05.HTML

A profile of Italian dictator Benito Mussolini.

HTTP://WWW.FORDHAM.EDU/HALSALL/MOD/MODSBOOK45.HTML

This site offers excerpts from important speeches, news reports, and documents of the World War II era.

HTTP://WWW.BBC.CO.UK/HISTORY/WAR/WWTWO/JAPAN_QUEST_EMPIRE_01.SHTML

This site describes Japan's efforts to build an empire in the Pacific.

HTTP://FCIT.COEDU.USF.EDU/HOLOCAUST/RESOURCE/GALLERY/NR1939.HTM

Part of a teacher's guide to the Holocaust, this site contains a photo gallery of the German invasion of Poland.

Numbers in **bold italics** refer to captions.

PICTURE CREDITS

ABOUT THE AUTHOR

JIM CORRIGAN has authored numerous newspaper and magazine articles, as well as several nonfiction books for students. A full-time freelance writer, Corrigan specializes in topics relating to history, travel, and ethnic studies. He has studied the World War II era for more than two decades. His other books for young readers include *The Civil War in the West, Europeans and Native Americans, and Filipino Immigration*. He is currently writing a book on the Civil War's Battle of the Crater. He is a graduate of Penn State University and currently resides near Harrisburg, Pennsylvania.